Making dolls

Sunnhild Reinckens

Making dolls

Floris Books

Translated by Donald Maclean

First published in German under the title *Selbstgemachte
Puppen* and *Puppen zum Erzählen und Liebhaben*
by Hobbybücher, Pelikan, Hanover
First published in English in 1989 by Floris Books
Third impression 1997

British Library CIP Data available

ISBN 0-86315-093-4

Printed in the Netherlands

Contents

Foreword

It is a basic need of every child to have a little doll to love. Such a doll should be really soft, washable and its expression childlike and loveable, unlike the stiff, adult expression of most modern dolls.

With proper instructions it is not too difficult to make a doll yourself. After years of experience I know that anyone with a little skill, imagination and interest can succeed.

A doll made with loving care has a special value for the development of the child. It can become a faithful companion for many years during childhood — whether it be the soft doll for a baby or the large doll of the older child.

These dolls do not have a completed and perfected appearance, and are made of soft material. These qualities seem to arouse feelings of tenderness and care in the heart of the child. In contrast to dolls made of plastic which often appear cold and hard these dolls are round and cuddly, equally suited for boys and girls.

Experience has taught me that boys as much as girls like to play with dolls. The idea that you must not give a boy a doll is fortunately outmoded and it is more generally seen that doll-play can contribute to a boy's development into a loving father.

I made a doll some fifteen years ago for a three-year-old boy. He called her Mary and they were inseparable. Mary kept him company throughout his childhood and was subjected to endless washing and mending. The boy was an only child and Mary was both 'daughter' and 'sister'. Often mothers have spoken of the care and tenderness which this kind of soft, home-made doll calls forth in children, and how children are comforted by them when they are sick or in trouble.

The hearts of children and of adults too are open to these dolls who speak specially to old and ill people, and it is hardly surprising that in old people's homes and in nursing homes the making of dolls is encouraged as a therapy.

Given that the doll is so important for the child and especially because it is an idealized picture of the human being for small children it is better if they do not witness the process of doll-making. The doll for children must be a whole and not a head by itself or bits of arms and legs, so it is preferable to make the doll when they are not present.

Use only good material for making toys: cotton, good wool for the hair and pure fleece wool or woollen mixture for stuffing. Try not to use artificial materials, for a good doll should be made of 'real' material.

Patterns and sizes are shown with the instructions. They can of course be varied and adapted as can materials.

Fifteen years ago I had the good fortune to be introduced to these dolls by Lieselotte Bosse, a teacher at the Waldorf School in Hanover, and to work with her for some time. What I learned there I have been able to pass on to many other women; and for that I am very grateful to Frau Bosse.

Now to doll-making.

1. Making the doll's head

The most important thing when making dolls is that the head should be exactly right. If it is not made correctly it can look deformed or too old. It is, in fact, not at all difficult to make a really good head, and with a little skill and practice you will soon be able to make all kinds of heads with the help of the drawing and instructions which follow.

Look at a child's head from the side and you will notice the beautifully rounded forehead, the round often chubby cheeks and the usually tiny nose. The dolls I describe look just as sweet with or without a nose. If you do make a nose make sure it is small and stumpy so that the doll does not look too old. If the nose is too round or too long it will make the face look grown-up or like a Punch.

The head is formed by tying two important lines: first the line of the eyes, and secondly the line of the cheeks. The depressions caused by tying these lines will give shape and definition to the finished head.

The first set of instructions are for a medium-sized doll.

Materials:
Tubular gauze 2¼″ (6 cm) wide, from which we cut a piece 10″ (25 cm) long, strong linen thread, about 1½ oz (40 g) good well-teased sheep's wool, smooth pink knitted cotton, sewing materials and glue.

Tubular gauze bandages can be bought in various sizes from a chemist and are ideal for this purpose as they are strong and stretchable and woven round. For smaller dolls it is better to cut a piece of tubular bandage lengthwise.

Instructions:
The length needed depends on the size of the doll to be made: the tube must be of such a length that we can make the head and body from it.

First turn the tube inside out and wind a thread several times tightly round it at one end and tie tight. Trim the knot (Fig. 1). Turn the bandage right side out again (Fig. 2) to make a bag. Stuff about 1½ oz (40 g) fleece-wool into this bag, packing it in firmly to make a ball as big as a tangerine or small apple. Tease a little wool out into the neck. Holding the 'head-ball' firmly in your left hand, with your right hand wind a strong thread tightly round the neck several times and tie. If you have not got enough wool in the neck the head will wobble, so pay attention to the neck (see Fig. 3).

If the smallest available size of tubular bandage is still too big for little dolls, use a piece of knitted cotton. Put a tight ball of fleece-wool into this and tie up tightly.

It is important that the head is neither too soft nor too hard; check by pressing; it should give only just a little.

Squeeze the head to an oval egg-shape before

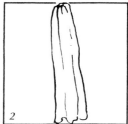

you start tying up. Take a long strong thread (about 45", 120 cm). Wind one end two or three times round the little finger of your left hand to stop the thread from slipping when you are tying up. Take the head also in your left hand. With your right hand now grasp the thread just beyond where it is wound round your little finger and wind it three times round the middle of the head tightly enough to make a depression along the line of the eyes. This needs some practice: the thread should be neither too tight nor too loose, and the line must not be too high. Now take the thread off your little finger and tie it with a treble knot at the side of the head (Fig. 4)

There should still be a lot of thread left over. Take it over the top of the head, and down to where the neck is tied. Wind it tightly twice round the neck, and take it back up like a chin-strap or a bonnet-string, and tie it again at the same place at the side, so that you now have six tight knots there. There should still be enough thread to thread a needle. Sew up both sides tightly three times where the threads cross at the ears (Fig. 5). The main job is now finished and the head has been divided into four parts, only the back of the head remains to be done, but this is not difficult. As the crossing points of the threads have been secured, the first thread can now be pulled down to the back of the neck. The wool will now be pushed up by the thread and held in position from below. This forms the back of the head (Fig. 6). If you now compare the doll's head with a child's head you will see that this method of tying up gives it the same basic shape.

If you don't want to make a nose you can now cover the head with knitted cotton, but if you do want one, it must be made at this stage.

Nose: Just below the 'eye-line' and in the very middle of the face, using a darning-needle or your finger-tips, tease out a little round lump of stuffing under the gauze. Gather round this lump with a fine needle and fine thread, draw tight and sew up. Don't make the nose too big or you will distort the face, too small and it will be unnoticeable. If the nose turns out to be too big take the thread out again and make the bobble smaller (Fig. 7)

If the nose is right gather round once more and secure.

Now smear some glue over the nose (just as if you were applying a thin layer of skin-cream to your own nose). When it hardens it helps keep the shape.

The nose can easily become worn and torn because the face covering is pulled so tightly over it. One can stick a bit of adhesive plaster over the nose before pulling the 'skin' over it. This reduces the chance of it wearing out.

The 'skin' consists of a rectangular piece of pink knitted cotton (or an appropriate skin colour) about ¾" (2 cm) wider than the head and 1–1½" (3–4 cm) longer than the head so that it can be pulled tightly around and pinned at the back of the head. Pull the covering well over the head.

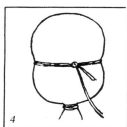

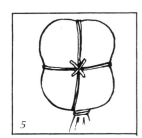

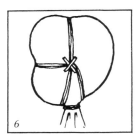

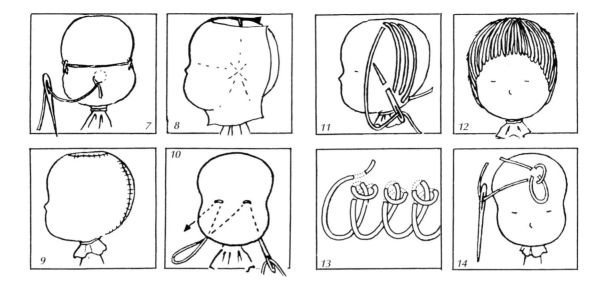

Overlap the corners tightly at the neck (Figs. 8 and 9). Make sure that you sew right into the stuffing so that the 'skin' does not come off like a bonnet. Always start sewing at the crown of the head and finish by winding and securing the thread tightly round the neck. There should be no creases.

The **eye-sockets:** The actual eyes are embroidered, but first stick two round-headed pins in to mark where the eyes are going to be. They should be right on the eye-line. Make sure that they are equidistant from the centre, not too close together and not too far apart. The pins must be stuck exactly through the eye-line thread. Thread a long, sharp needle. Anchor the end of the thread firmly to the left side of the head. Then thrust the needle diagonally through the head from the anchor so that it comes out at the left eye. Push it in again 1/10" (2 mm) further along, thrusting it once again diagonally through the head to come out on the right side. Pull the thread so that it makes a little hollow. Thrust the needle in again so that it comes out at the

pinhead of the right eye, where again you make a little hollow in the same way. Finally the needle comes out on the opposite side of the head (Fig. 10). Secure firmly so that the eyes don't come undone again. Chinese, Japanese and Eskimo dolls have slightly slanting eyes. Now the doll has much more shape and is coming to life.

2. Different hair styles

All these dolls have their hair sewn on. To sew in the hair it is best to use the embroidery stitch called the 'loop-stitch'. With a soft pencil, mark the hair-outline on the head so that you can see how far down to bring the hair. Mark the top of the head. Sew in from the crown round and downwards with long loops (Fig. 11). The first stitches should not be too close together, but leave a little space in between which is filled up when you go round the second time. For a full head of hair it may well be necessary to go round the head three or four times to make sure that the covering is not showing any

more (Fig. 12). If you want to make a boy's head with straight short hair keep to a straight line; but if the hair is to be looser and to look more natural make the hair-outline a bit more wavy. This loop-stitch is suitable for baby-dolls and boy-dolls.

To make a **mop of hair** or curly-head needs more time. Patience is especially required for the mop, but the result is worth the extra trouble. Stitch in the whole head with loose loops, each loop being tied in (Figs. 13 and 14). Begin at the outside edge and work upwards and inwards in a spiral to the crown (Fig. 15). Finally cut all the loops through. The head can be held over steam so that the wool, becomes more fuzzy and looks more like real hair. Then trim the hair. Such a hair-style admirably suits a boy-doll with a snub nose and freckles (Fig. 16). Make sure that the stitches go deeply into the head, so that the wool does not tear loose.

A **curly-head** is somewhat simpler. Make loops as in the mop, but as the loops are not cut through it is not necessary to tie in each loop. It is enough to tie in every fourth or fifth loop (Fig. 17). For an African doll the loops must be small and thick.

The final effect is more natural when the loops are brought right over the head and the intervals are filled up later. Some little curls on the forehead always look pretty.

A piece of fleece is excellent as a wig, especially if it is from a very curly or long-haired sheep. In order to get the right proportions cut a pattern from a paper serviette or a piece of pattern-paper which you fold over the head (we shall come back to this later). Now make a kind of 'fur-cap' with the wool inside. This is later turned inside out. Pucker the lower border with strong thread and try the whole thing over the head. If it fits well you can remove the thread.

Apply adhesive to the inside of the wig and stick it

firmly on the head so that some loose curls fall over the forehead from underneath. If the wig is too big the forehead easily becomes too low. This should be avoided. Finally as a precaution sew the wig on firmly. Every doll-maker likes to let the imagination run riot with girl's hair-styles. It is fun to see how the facial expression changes with a different hair-style. I do not recommend ready-made wigs since they cannot be fixed on satisfactorily.

Fluffy mohair-wool is also very suitable for doll's hair, but it is more difficult to find a suitable darning needle: long, sharp, with an eye big enough to take thick woollen yarn. I advise using the yarn double to make a full foundation.

To get a good, full **fringe** make a double row of loops hanging down over the forehead and cut them through later. Now overlap the fringe lightly with a 'loop-stitch' with which we make the rest of the hair. In this way it looks as if the fringe is coming

from below, which makes it look nice and natural (Fig. 18).

To make a **pony tail** we need long hair, of course, just as we shall for a bun, a crown or plaits. Mark the crown with a pin or a pencil and cover in the whole head with loop-stitches, leaving the loops of wool hanging down at the crown, so that in the end you can bunch the hair at the back. If the bunch

turns out to be too thin you can sew in some more yarn (Fig. 18).

To get a **bun** twist the hair tightly together, and pin it firmly to the top of the head and then sew it on firmly with little strong stitches (Fig. 19)

For a **crown** plait the hair first and then lay it as a crown round the head and sew on with strong stitches.

To make long hair for **plaiting:** begin with loop-stitches from the top of the head as already described (Fig. 12) or with a pencil trace the line of a parting which runs over the whole head from the neck to the top and from the top to the fringe. On each side of the head a bit lower than the ear mark a point with the pencil. Fill the head from the parting to the ears with loop-stitches. Not all the stitches should come out at the ears otherwise you will get a lump. Try to get the stitches evenly distributed. First have a good look at a child with plaits.

Once the head is well covered with hair in this

way we can begin with loose hanging hair. For this take doubled yarn and anchor it at the ear. Then make long loops, slightly longer than the plaits are to be. Anchor the loops in the same way as the little loops were secured for the mop (Fig. 13). Make the loops on each side of the head in the same way. Once the bunches of hair are thick and long enough secure the yarn and cut through the loops. Now the hair can be plaited. The plaits can then if desired be wound up and fixed on firmly (Figs. 20 and 21).

3. Painting the face

Materials:
Good quality coloured pencils, a red wax crayon, pen and nib, blue, red, brown and white textile colours.

Instructions:
Now that the head is finished one can begin to give it a facial expression. Many people are afraid to tackle this, but it is not that difficult if you practice first on a bit of material.

It is most important to have the two eyes and the mouth forming an equilateral triangle (Fig. 22).

Mark these three points lightly with textile colours. First shake the colour well so that some sticks to the lid. Dip a fine nib into the colour in the lid and make a round dot in the eye-hole and gradually increase its size. The eyes can be elongated to the left and right (Fig. 23).

Take a sharp pencil and trace the outline of the mouth round the tip of the triangle, then paint in the

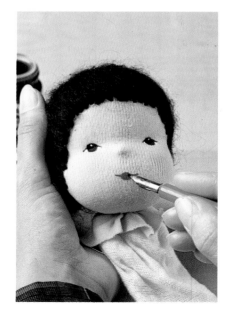

mouth with red textile colour. I cannot over-stress the need to be sparing with the colour. An over-painted face will lose its childlike quality. Take a red pencil, crayon or piece of pink chalk and colour the cheeks.

A **simple baby-face** is always sweet and loveable.

A freckled rather **cheeky,** grinning little girl can be given more expression by applying a little white colouring *very* carefully to the corners of the eyes with a fine nib, and putting a little white dot in the pupils.

The mouth and eyes of **dark-skinned** dolls should be given a foundation layer of white. Once this is dry the black or brown for the eyes and the red for the mouth can be applied.

Freckles are simply some dots round the nose applied with a fine nib.

Textile colours have many advantages for this kind of work. The most important is that the doll can be washed, although it may be necessary to repaint the cheeks now and again. On the other hand because textile colours are so durable they must be handled carefully. You cannot correct what has been painted wrongly, so it is recommended that you always make a pencil outline first.

4. Cuddly doll

Having learnt how to make a doll's head by tying up, how to make a face and sew in the hair, we can start on our first real doll. This is called a 'cuddly doll,' and is the best model for learning to make the body. Once this is understood it can be adapted to many of the other kinds of doll.

The baby's suit for this doll can be knitted or sewn.

Material:
Tubular gauze 1½" (4 cm) wide and about 6" (14–15 cm) long for the head and body, fleece wool, pink knitted cotton, woollen cloth or terry-towelling for the skin, knitting wool.

Instructions
Form the head with about 1 oz (25 g) wool completely to the hair stage, as described above. The body is always one and a half times as long as the head, and must never be wider than the head. By pressing in the sides you can give the body shoulders, but mind that you do not make a hunchback!

Fill the tube which hangs down from the head with stuffing (wool). Tuck the ends in and sew up tight. Make sure that the wool is stuffed tightly right in up to the neck otherwise there will be a space and the head will be floppy (Fig. 24). Now make a furrow down each side of the body and pin it tight (Fig. 25). Push the wool up with your forefinger to make a shoulder. Sew up the furrow and sew the remainder of the head covering on to the chest and back. This gives the head more support (Fig. 26).

Make the baby's suit as shown on the pattern (Fig. 28). Scale up the pattern and cut two pattern pieces from a soft woollen cloth or terry-towelling. Good pieces from an old jersey or sweater in a nice soft colour are very suitable.

Sew up the suit, stitching the arms as far as the dotted lines on the pattern. Leave a neck opening. Leave the cuffs open so that the hands can be sewn in. Sew up the seams tightly under the arms, legs and feet, either by hand or on the sewing-machine. Turn the suit inside out and fill the legs with wool, but not too stiffly. Now insert the body into the suit by the neck opening taking care that the head is in the middle. Pin the head firmly on to the suit and sew the shoulders right up to the neck. Then sew

24

25

26

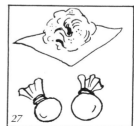
27

the suit firmly round the neck with little stitches. Turn under a small hem on the outside edge of the sleeves and tack with strong thread. Then stuff the arms in the same way as the legs.

Hands. Roll some teased wool together to make a tight ball. Lay each ball on a piece of knitted cotton 1¼" (3 cm) square and tie up tight with thread. Trim off the surplus material (Fig. 27). Insert the hands into the cuffs, draw the tacking thread tight and secure. Sew round once more tightly into the material. For the feet tack a single thread about 1" (2—3 cm) above the underside of the legs; draw a little and secure.

You can add an apron as in the pattern.

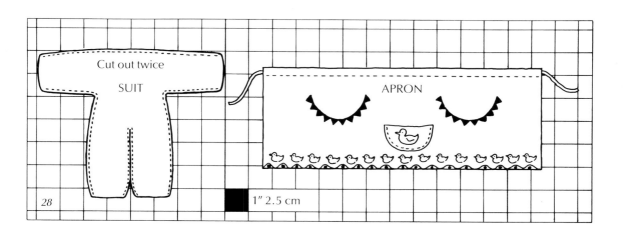

Cut out twice

SUIT

APRON

28

1" 2.5 cm

5. A doll for very little children

Many children need something soft to cuddle in bed before they go to sleep. Very often they will use a piece of cloth wound round their fingers. The doll that we are now going to make meets this comfort need. It is specially suitable for babies under eight months old and is intended to lie beside them in bed. I like to make it from a bag loosely stuffed with fleece wool, but some people prefer to make the doll firmer like a little cushion.

Materials:
Tubular gauze 2¼" (6 cm) wide, cut to 10" (25 cm) length, for the head and body, fleece wool and pink knitted cotton for the head, a soft piece of knitted cotton for the body.

Instructions:
First make a head from the tube-bandage. A nose in this case is not necessary. Then loosely stuff the body with teased wool, making it one and a half times as long as the head.

Scale up the pattern and cut out the pieces. Gather the waist of the two pieces of the lower half and sew onto the upper half. Sew right around, leaving the cuffs open. Push the body through the neck opening and close it, sewing the body firmly on to the outer garment. Trim the seams with lace or braid. Make the hands as for the Cuddly Doll (Fig. 27). Loosely stuff the arms and sew the hands on.

The cap from the pattern can be added.

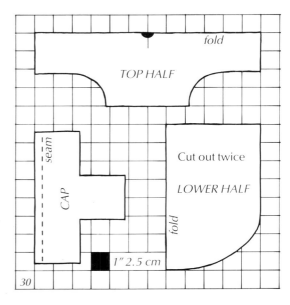

6. Printed cotton or corduroy baby-doll

31

In the photograph opposite you will see three dolls made from similar patterns and put together in much the same way but which look very different. These kinds of doll are very suitable for little children and babies. The corduroy doll is stiffer and more robust. It can even stand up by itself because it is firmly stuffed, while the cotton doll is soft and cuddly and is intended as a doll for little children to cuddle when they are going to sleep.

Materials:
Tubular gauze 2¼" (6 cm) wide, cut to 10" (25 cm) length, for the head and body. Fleece wool for stuffing. Pink knitted cotton, knitting wool and a piece of cotton cloth or corduroy.

Instructions:
Make the head from the tube. The cotton doll has hair of loops coming out from under her cap. Do not use mohair wool for dolls for babies as this sheds hairs which can get into the baby's mouth. Scale up the pattern to the right size and cut it out of cotton cloth or corduroy.

Sew the trousers, gather them around the waist. The creases of the trousers should be distributed evenly round the doll and the trousers sewn firmly on to the jacket (the top half in the pattern). Stuff the legs and then push the body through the neck opening. The trouser-band must sit exactly round the middle of the body.

As mentioned, the corduroy doll must be stuffed much more tightly than the cotton doll so that it gets

a proper soft stomach, but for both dolls the proportions remain the same: the body is one and a half times as long as the head.

You can dress the corduroy doll in a smock or apron. In my experience this is the child's first real 'playmate'.

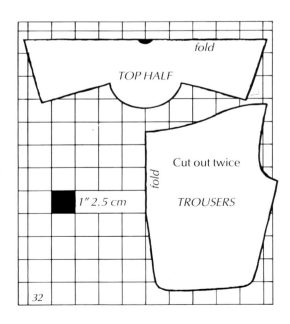

fold

TOP HALF

Cut out twice

fold

1" 2.5 cm

TROUSERS

32

7. Knitted doll: Pippi Longstocking

The dolls described here are intended for older children; they can be dressed and undressed. These knitted dolls can be made in any size as long as the proportions are maintained. From the shoulders to the feet should be three to three and a half times the length of the head. The body and legs are knitted and if this is done with coloured wools or cotton then the doll has a vest and tights on right away (Fig. 33).

Material:
Tubular gauze 2¼" (6 cm) wide and 10" (25 cm) long, fleece wool, pink knitted cotton, knitting wool of various colours, pieces of knitted cotton or woollen cloth, leather for shoes.

Instructions:
Make the head from the tube. Give the face a cheeky, turned up nose and make red pigtails that stick out. Tightly stuff the remaining tube which forms the body (1½ times as long as the head), then sew the head covering on to the body so that the head does not wobble.

The arms are made from strips of knitted cotton 6" × 2" (15 × 5 cm) folded lengthwise and sewn to form a tube. Round off the hands. Stuff them tightly leaving about ⅜" (1 cm) without filling at the top. Hem this piece and sew the arms firmly on to the shoulders (Fig. 34). Make sure that the arms don't stick out; they should hang down loosely reaching to the hips. When raised they should reach to the crown of the head. To make the hands tack round the arm with little stitches. Draw up the tacking thread and secure firmly.

Knit the body-suit which consists of a vest and tights as shown in Fig. 33. Cast on stitches for a width of 6¼" (16 cm) (you can make a trial piece) and knit 4" (10 cm) with stocking stitch (one row plain, one row purl). Then continue the legs each on a separate needle to a total length of 10¼" (26 cm), and cast off.

Fold over the legs lengthwise and sew up along the inside of the leg, sew on to the back of the vest and close the bottom of the legs.

Alternatively, you can sew the suit of this doll using knitted cotton or a light woollen cloth. Take

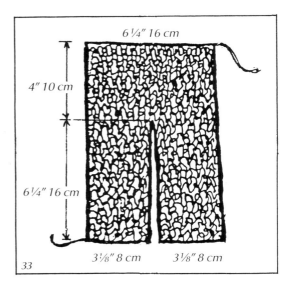

into account whether the material will stretch, in order to prevent the doll turning out too thick or too thin once it is stuffed with wool. Knitted cotton is best used longitudinally and sewn with a small zigzag stitch. This doll's body is about 10" (26 cm) tall and about 3" (7–8 cm) wide.

Once the body is sewn together turn the good side out and stuff the body and legs firmly.

To make the legs more moveable and to make it easier to bend the feet forward, before stuffing stick pins in at the groin and ankles through one thickness of the material (Fig. 35). In this way a space is left. When the whole doll is well stuffed sew across the line of the pins so that no more wool can get past. To make the feet, bend in the bottom of the legs and sew the bend.

The whole suit, whether knitted or sewn, consists of the vest and tights. Pull this right up to the neck and if necessary stuff a little more loose wool into the stomach. Pin the suit on to the neck.

Turn the doll over so that she is lying on her stomach. Form a bottom by stuffing in two clumps of wool under her suit. Pin the suit on at the neck and sew the shoulders (Fig. 36). Finally sew on the suit round the neck and under the arms with little stitches. It is possible to make a neck from a piece of knitted cotton ¾" (2 cm) broad which is then sewn on to the body and the head, this gives extra firmness.

Pippi's appearance is completed by a typical dress (Fig. 37) and various coloured stockings and shoes.

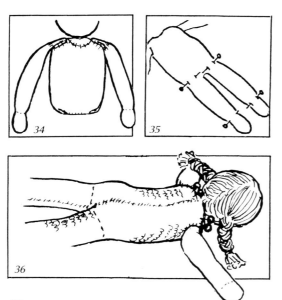

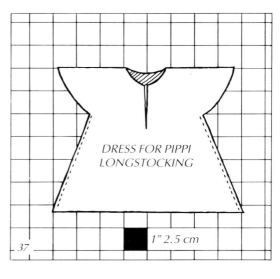

DRESS FOR PIPPI LONGSTOCKING

1" 2.5 cm

8. Baby-dolls

Children are particularly fond of baby-dolls which seem to call for special tenderness and care. It is as if the children in play bring the doll to life and make it the companion of their childhood.

The large baby in the photograph on page 28 was specially made for my thirteen-year-old daughter who specially wanted it. It was to be like a real baby and was to have the same weight.

Once the head was sewn up I filled a plastic bag with fine sand, tied it tightly with adhesive tape to prevent any sand from running out, inserted it in the body and packed fleece wool around it. The arms and legs were, of course, stuffed with wool so that the doll remained soft and cuddly although it had a realistic weight.

This doll is suitable only for older children because it cannot be washed and is quite heavy. You can adjust the pattern to the size of doll you want. The width of the tubular bandage can vary from 2¼" to 4" (6 to 10 cm). The measurements of the pattern are for a doll with a 2¼" (6 cm) hose-bandage.

Materials:
Tubular gauze and a piece of knitted cotton for the head, fleece wool, pieces of cloth, mohair wool for the hair.

Instructions:
Make a bag for the body as in the pattern (Fig. 38). Cut four each of the arm and leg shapes using the patterns in Figs. 39 and 40. Sew the pairs of cut-outs together. The seams of the legs and feet lie in front and behind to accentuate the width of the feet.

All dolls with sewn-up bodies require the length of the tubular gauze left over after the head is filled not to be too great otherwise it will not easily go through the neck opening of the body.

The piece of tube must be tightly stuffed with wool to prevent the head from wobbling.

Fill the body about half full with the bag of sand, then push the neck piece through the neck opening.

Stuff the rest of the body and shoulders with

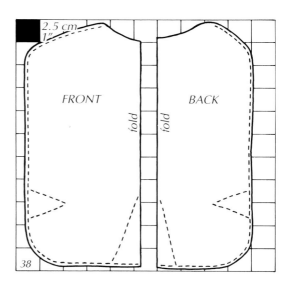

2.5 cm
1"

FRONT   fold   fold   BACK

38

27

wool. Sew the neck firmly on to the head with a little hem just above the neck-seam.

Fill the arms and legs, stuffing the wool right down into the hands and feet. Sew them up. Sew them on to the shoulders and hips respectively and try to ensure that the legs and arms can move. Try to achieve a typical baby posture (see Figs. 38–41).

For a baby-doll's hair use good mohair wool, work on to the head with a flat loop-stitch.

9. John and Tim, dolls for dressing and undressing

These two jolly lovable dolls are for dressing. Tim is a black boy and has a suit of dark-coloured knitted cotton. John has sewn-on arms and legs (Figs. 42 and 43). Both have curly hair wigs made of fur that look real. It may be possible to buy remnants from a furrier.

Tim has a round face like all the other dolls, tied at the neck, as already described, but to make John look more of a cheery rogue we have given him a more formed chin and cheeks (see also pages 44–45).

You can darken Tim's skin with textile colours. You can use washed light-coloured knitted cotton

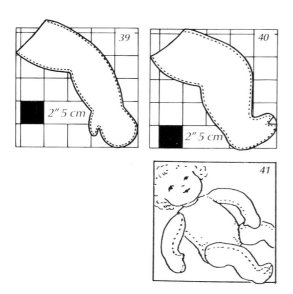

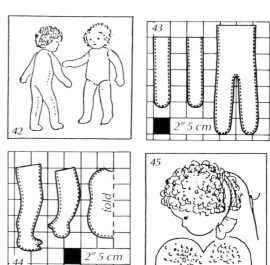

(old T-shirts for instance). With a black-coloured doll eyes and mouth show up better on a white foundation, so it is essential first to give eyes and mouth a double priming of white, which must dry thoroughly before overpainting the black or brown of the eyes and the red of the mouth.

Materials:
Tubular gauze 2¼" (6 cm) wide, 8"–8½" (20–22 cm) long, knitted cotton, fur, fleece wool, strong thread and sewing things including a leather-needle and razor or scalpel.

Instructions:
Tim: Make the body and legs from one piece (Fig. 43), as described in the method for the knitted doll (page 24). Again the body is one and a half times as long as the head.

Sew the arms and stuff them. Pull the body part right up to the neck, pin on and sew on.

Bend the feet up and sew across the bend.

John: Make the head and body as described for the baby-doll and fit well into the neck-opening of the body covering.

Make the arms and legs according to the pattern (see Fig. 44), stuff them, sew them up and fasten them on to the shoulders and hips.

To make a wig first you will need a pattern. Put a piece of paper over the head as if you were making a cap, cut away the edges and so make a shape as in Fig. 45 to form a basic wig. Now place the pattern on the back of the fur-skin and cut out the shape with the razor or scalpel. Note that nearly all furs have hair lying in a certain direction, and take this into account when cutting out the wigs. It is best to let the hair fall over the forehead.

First sew the two seams at the back of the piece with the skin to the outside to form a cap. Be careful not to sew in lumps of fur or to pull the wrong side through. Turn the wig inside out so that the furry side is to the outside, tack around the wig at the brim. Apply glue to the inside of the wig. Set it on the head and, once the wig is sitting correctly, pull the tacking thread tight. Stitch on firmly.

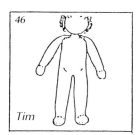

46   Tim

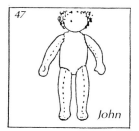

47   John

10. Tiny baby-doll

The baby-doll which we are now going to make has moveable arms which can be bent to shape.

Materials:
A piece of tubular gauze or knitted cotton, insulated or gardening wire, fleece wool, woollen or terry-towelling.

Instructions:
It is not always possible to get narrow tubular bandages under 2¼" (3 cm) width, but you can use a piece of knitted cotton to make a head of ⅜"–¾" (1–2 cm). Make the head and body in the same way as the hands on page 17 (Fig. 27). Make the arms by taking a piece of wire about 12" (30 cm) long. Wind the middle of the wire a few times round the neck and allow the ends to stick out. Bend the ends back round. Wrap a tuft of fleece wool round the ends and cover with a cloth about ⅜" × ⅜" (1 cm × 1 cm). Bind the cloth on with strong thread; this makes the hands. Now wind the fleece wool round the arms. Wind thread round the wool to keep it in place (Fig. 49).

Now make a bag of woollen or cotton cloth (see pattern, Fig. 48) to form the body which should be quite even. If there are lumps or pits anywhere some loose fleece wool can be stuffed in to even the stuffing out. At the neck turn the seam inwards, then the bag can be sewn on.

The arms stick right out on each side. Sew the material under the arms particularly tightly to make a short bodice (Fig. 50).

Finally the bag can be tricked out with coloured bands or ribbons. You can also clothe the doll in a

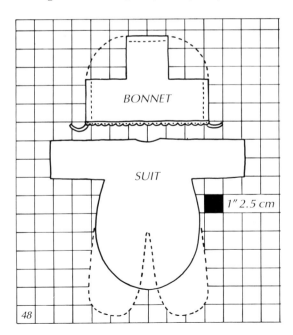

BONNET

SUIT

1" 2.5 cm

48

49

50

51 *52*

christening dress made of lace. A little lace cap then completes this outfit (Fig. 52).

Using the same pattern you can make dolls with cut–out arms and legs without the wire frame. This doll will then be soft and floppy so that it can be really cuddled, and is more suitable for younger children (Fig. 51).

A doll with a wire frame is naturally meant for older children and not for very little ones.

11. Finger puppets

If you watch a baby in his cot playing with his fingers and making happy noises you see the beginnings of the finger games which are encouraged further in the kindergarten. The child's speech-development is undoubtedly helped by finger movements so it is important to preserve and cultivate the old finger-rhymes. An advancement of these finger games can be seen in the finger puppets which can make up the first and smallest theatre, and with which we can speak, sing, explain and act. Old nursery rhymes and games can be brought

53

to life, as for example Jack and Jill, Sing a Song of Sixpence or Little Bo-Peep.

Materials:
Scraps of knitted cotton, fleece wool, scraps of felt, fur or sheepskin, 1″ (2–3 cm) wide elastic.

Instructions:
For these little dolls it is not necessary to make a head from a tube first. Simply lay a little ball of fleece wool on a square piece of knitted cotton 3″ (8 cm) square and tie it up tightly underneath. Trim the material straight so that there is still about ½″ (1–1.5 cm) hanging below the head. Make a nice round head taking care that there are no creases (Fig. 54).

Wrap some elastic round your finger to make a roll, and sew the elastic roll on to the neck (Fig. 55). Take a piece of cloth 6″–8″ (15–20 cm) wide and 4″ (10 cm) long, and sew the short ends together. Along the top edge make a little hem, gather it and sew it firmly on to the head (Fig. 56).

Draw the face with a fine pencil line and indent the eye-sockets from behind the head with a needle and thread. These dolls can be given a tiny nose by tacking round a little lump, gathering and securing. A witch's nose must be made a bit bigger. By changing the shape of the nose you can completely alter the doll's character. It is great fun working out the personality of the doll, accentuating particular traits, designing different hair styles and clothes. Give faces to the dolls with a fine nib or a paintbrush using textile colours.

Of course finger puppets can be made in the same way as other dolls, with tied and shaped heads (see pages 7–10), but for finger games this is hardly necessary.

You can assemble a proper little puppet-theatre, pack it in a little box and take it with you to use when you are waiting at the doctor's or in the hospital or on a long journey. Skill and imagination are developed and the child can make the little figures dance on his hand, talk and tell stories.

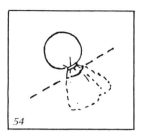

54

55

56

12. A little table-theatre

Children are most intensively involved in fairy tales at the age of four or five. Tell the stories calmly and faithfully and do not overact. Soon the child will want to hear the same story over and over again, beginning to absorb the wealth of imagery and to develop a feeling for the underlying justice in the story without being disturbed by the occasional medieval blood-thirstiness.

A brightly coloured box of puppets enables the child to tell favourite fairy-tales and act them before other children. The child sits absorbed at an improvised stage furnished with things provided from the household: cloths, flower-pots, pegs, and so on. At one and the same time the child is narrator, stage-director, actor and audience, with brothers and sisters, friends, parents and relations being drawn into the magic of the play.

Materials:
Fleece wool, knitted cotton, tubular gauze 1¼" (3 cm) wide, bits of cloth for the costumes, insulated wire, a base (a jam-jar lid, a little saucer or stiff cardboard disc).

Instructions:
Make a doll's head from the hose-bandage or from a piece of knitted cotton, and a body as shown on page 32. Give the doll the hair style that best suits its role. Unlike the finger-puppets these dolls must be able to stand, so they need a firm base to prevent them from falling when they are moved. The arms should be able to move so that they can carry a basket or a baby. That is why they have a wire base. Take some insulated wire 10–12" (25–30 cm) long, a bit stronger than gardening wire, or two or three fine wires twisted like rope. Wind the wire round the neck (Fig. 57), wrap the arms round with fleece wool and secure with thread. Sew the arms firmly on to the shoulders. Cut the arms to the right length and arrange them in the right gesture. Little balls of wool sewn up in a piece of cloth make the hands (see Fig. 27, page 17). Now you can take the measurements for the clothes. Sleeves for jackets and blouses are best drawn over the arms first, and sewn on at the wrist and shoulder. Then the front and back parts can be put on and sewn on to the body and the sleeves. The skirt should be made of

57

58

59

60

stiff material so that the doll will stand. Gather at the waist and sew on to the body (Fig. 58).

When stuffing be careful not to make these dolls too stout, but at the same time remember that they must be stiff enough to stand up. Once the doll is stuffed, close the skirt underneath with the lid, covering it with a round piece of cloth and sew up (Fig. 59)

With this table-theatre lots of stories and fairy tales can be told while the children themselves set up the scenery and move the puppets.

13. Punch-in-the-Cone and stick-puppets

These puppets can surprise and please because they are so versatile. If a child is hurt or is being difficult then Punch-in-the-Cone can soon put matters right. Just let Punch peep cautiously over the edge of the cone, then come out altogether and make a few turns while he says some comforting or cheering words. Then perhaps he hops back in again, peeps out once more, comes right out … and soon your child is laughing and has forgotten the upset.

Materials:
A piece of dowelling 20–24" (50–60 cm) long ¼" (6 mm) diameter, glue, tubular gauze (1¼", 3 cm wide), knitted cotton cloths, fur and a little bell.

Instructions:
Make the head as usual. Apply a thick coat of glue to one end of the stick and insert it into the head. Twist it round several times so that the wool sticks firmly to the stick. Tie securely at the neck and wrap the rest of the tube tightly round the stick so that the head sits firmly on the stick (Fig. 61). Make a cocky nose (see Fig. 7 on page 10).

Put a piece of knitted cotton over the head and

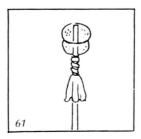

61

62

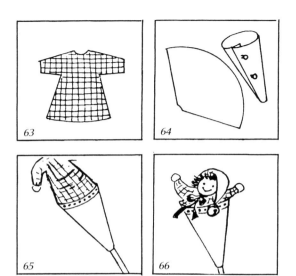

63

64

65

66

cover it. Make a border of curly hair round it and put a pointed cap on top so that the hair peeps out from below it (Fig. 62).

Then give Punch his jacket, gather it in at the neck and sew (Fig. 63).

To make the cone: Cut out a cardboard disc with a radius just over twice the diameter of Punch's jacket. Divide the disc into three segments. Discard two segments and make a cone of the third, sticking it together. You can use clips or sew it together till the glue sets (Fig. 64). Cover the cone with coloured paper or cloth. The bottom of Punch's jacket must be exactly of the same width as the top of the cone. If it does not quite fit you can let out or take in the seam of the jacket. Sew the bottom of the jacket on to the top of the cone. A braid or coloured band can cover the join (Figs. 65 and 66).

Simple stick-puppets are made in the same way as Punch but without the cone. They can be made bigger and more expressive than finger puppets.

Children between the ages of three and seven are able to play by themselves with the stick-puppets and can help to make them.

14. The gnome

As I have already mentioned in the foreword there are still parents who feel they cannot give their boys a doll to play with. However, when I talk to these mothers I can nearly always persuade them that this is a misconceived idea and that boys like playing with dolls just as much as girls. Very often then if the mother does decide to make a doll for her little son she will choose a gnome or a dwarf.

The photograph on page 43 shows two gnomes whose mischievous and puckish faces are made basically in the same way as earlier dolls, but with some refinements described below. For gnomes generally a simple nose is sufficient.

Materials:
Tubular gauze 2¼"–3" (6–8 cm) wide, 10–12½" (25–32 cm) length. A piece of fleece for the hair, fleece wool, pieces of knitted cotton, buttons and bells. A long, sharp needle, strong thread.

Instructions:
Make the gnomes in exactly the same way as the corduroy doll already described (page 22), but the suit now consists of a soft material. The larger gnome's suit is made of one piece, and the head is made of a tubular bandage.

The hair which sticks out from under the pointed hat is a piece of curly fleece first stuck on to the head and then sewn on. The pointed hat has a little bell at its tip. Before making the faces as already described (page 15) we shall need the long, sharp needle and good thread.

Make the **head** from the tubular bandage. Do not stuff the head too tightly, so that it can be given a better shape (see also Punch-in-the-Cone, page 40).

Make the nose as shown in Fig. 7 (page 10), then anchor the thread beside one nostril. Make a long loop along the corner of the mouth and backwards to where the hair starts. Pull the thread through and secure. The taut thread makes a furrow which brings out the cheek form. Now bring the thread back along the same way to the starting point. Now push the needle right through the nose to come out at the other nostril and repeat the sewing on that side (see top left photograph).

Tease up some wool with a sharp needle under the 'skin' of the cheeks to fill them out. Tease out the chin in the same way (top right photograph).

Indicate the outline of the mouth beforehand with some fine pencil marks. Anchor a thread behind the ear. Thrust the needle right through the head to the right-hand corner of the mouth, thence to the middle of the mouth and then right through the head again to behind the other ear. Repeat this but going to the other corner of the mouth and coming out again at the opposite side from before. Do not pull the thread too tight. The mouth now looks like a little triangle (see the two lower photographs).

The mouth can be made in a different way: above and below a straight stitch tease up some wool with a sharp needle so that it makes lips.

Finally smear all the sewn parts with glue. Then the 'skin' can be drawn over the head. If necessary you can give the contours emphasis from outside with a thick needle and set the lips with little stitches at the corners of the mouth.

Although it may sound rather complicated it is really quite easy. After some practice you will be surprised how much individual expression you can give each gnome or doll.

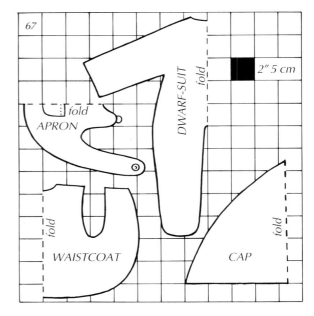

67

APRON · fold

DWARF-SUIT · fold

2" 5 cm

WAISTCOAT · fold

CAP · fold

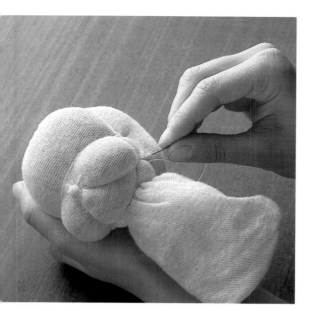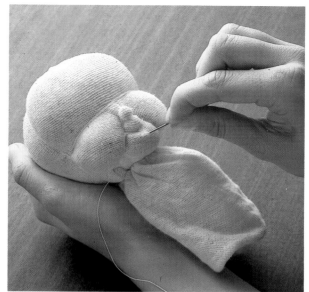

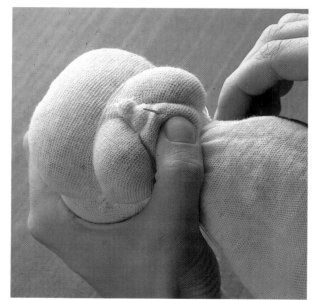

15. Snow-White and the seven dwarfs

Material:
Tubular gauze 2¼" (6 cm) wide, fleece wool, pieces of knitted cotton, black wool for Snow-White's hair and a gold head-band, the dwarfs have an insulated-wire frame, mohair wool for their beards, and pieces of felt.

Instructions:
Snow-White: Make a head from the tubular bandage, attach long black hair, make the body like the knitted dolls. She is dressed in a long white dress and wears a golden band in her hair like a princess. Snow-White lives in a little wooden house with the seven dwarfs.

Make the **dwarfs** in the same way as the cuddly dolls (page 17) but with a wire skeleton inside so that they can be bent. Their mohair wool beards are sewn on with a loop-stitch, or if made of bits of fur can be stuck on and then sewn on (Fig. 68). Make the dwarf's head and body but give him a pronounced nose to take away the baby face of the cuddly doll.

70

71

72

73

Now make the skeleton. Lay the neck on to the centre of a 3 ft (1 m) long insulated wire and loop the wire round the neck (as if strangling the gnome). Now wind the wire to form an arm on each side, and sew the sides on to the body. Wind the loose ends to form the legs, and finally twist the two ends together under the stomach. Sew into the stomach so that the sharp ends stick inward (Fig. 70).

Lay some fleece wool round this frame and bind on with strong thread. Sew the frame inside the body (Fig. 71). Make the hands with a ball of wool covered by a small piece of knitted cotton. Before drawing the outer body-suit over the inner body put some wool padding on the stomach and bottom and even out any lumps. Sew up the sleeves and neck openings with small stitches (Fig. 72). A pointed cap and a felt cloak (see Fig. 69) make these figures into jolly fairy-tale dwarfs. You can give the dwarfs waistcoats, aprons or little haversacks (Fig. 73).

68

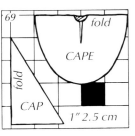
69   fold

CAPE

fold

CAP

1" 2.5 cm

16. Hänsel and Gretel

Here you see Hänsel and Gretel standing inquisitively at the ginger-bread house and nibbling at it. They are a little bigger than the doll's house figures (see page 52).

Materials:
Tubular gauze or knitted cotton 1¼" (3 cm) wide, 5½"–6" (14–15 cm) long, padded or insulated wire, strong thread, wool and knitted cotton.

Instructions:
Make the head and body with the tubular bandage, as described on page 32. Fill with wool and tie up. Bend a piece of the insulated or padded wire into a U-shape. Insert this into the body below the stomach to make the legs. Sew up the body.

Place another bit of padded wire behind the neck and bend the ends forward to make the arms. Sew the wire firmly on to the body. Check the proportions between body, arms and legs. If the limbs appear too long they can be shortened (Fig. 74).

Wind fleece wool round the arms and legs and secure with thread. Make the hands with a ball of wool covered with a piece of knitted cotton.

Bend the wire round twice for the feet so that the dolls stand firmly. Sew a piece of knitted cotton round the feet. Check the doll to make sure that no sharp points of wire are sticking out. They must be well covered with extra wool. Sew the material of the arms and legs firmly on to the body. The clothes are cut and sewn on to the body. These figures are

not meant for dressing and undressing, they belong exclusively to the story as Hänsel and Gretel.

In this way you can also make Christmas crib figures, but because the dolls represent adults give the faces more form and expression.

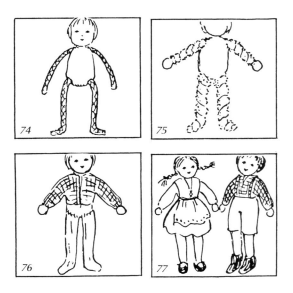

17. Grandma and Granddad. Dolls for adults and children

78

79

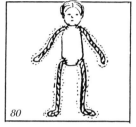

80

81

SOLE

In the photograph you can see 'story time' with Granddad and Grandma. Such dolls can be made as ornaments for adults as well as toys for children. For children grandparents embody warmth, protection and often a more indulgent way of child-rearing.

Perhaps this old-time granny, with her bun and her glasses slipping down her nose and her blue checked apron, will give you joy and awaken old memories. Her round apple-cheeked face expresses peace and goodness. She is an archetypal grandmother. A piece of the past is made present in these dolls for children and adults.

Materials:
Tubular gauze 2¼" (6 cm) wide, fleece wool, glue, pink knitted cotton, two hanks of grey wool, padded wire.

Instructions:
It is important to get a round kindly granny face. Make a round knobbly nose (Grandfather has a longer thinner one) with two cheek threads going from each side of the nose to the back of the head, then pull the cheeks and chin well out using a needle to tease the wool under the skin, and stretch a thread over where the mouth has been marked. If you pull too tight the mouth will look too toothless. If the loop-stitch has become too straight stitch the ends of the mouth outwards over the cheek-thread so that granny looks more friendly. Using a back-stitch sew some wrinkles on her forehead. Paint the

shaping with glue and cover with pink knitted cotton (Fig. 78).

For the hair use two skeins of grey unspun wool or thick knitting wool. Lay the first skein over the head from front to back and fasten at the neck. Lay the second sideways across the first. Make a parting in the middle. Plait the loose hair hanging down the neck, twist into a bun and sew on (Fig. 79).

The frame and body are made as for Hänsel and Gretel. You can use thick insulated wire, but padded wire is preferable.

Cover the arms and body with sewn knitted cotton arms and knitted or sewn outer body (see pages 29f).

Finally dress the dear old folk and put slippers on their feet.

18. The dolls' house and its inhabitants

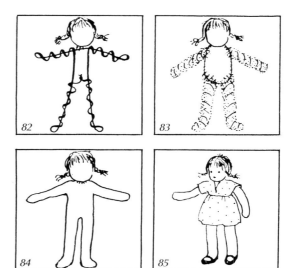

Here you see a cosy living-room painted blue with simple wooden furniture, and a family: father, mother, grandmother and two children playing. With these tiny flexible figures you can give a lot of pleasure to older children. Children identify with the various members of the family and use the dolls to play their parts. In my experience little boys often play intensively with the dolls' house and its inmates. I do not believe that only girls are interested in dolls' houses.

The creation of these dolls requires some skill and patience. The tiny proportions, the wire 'skeleton', and the sewing of the clothes mean a lot of very fine work.

Materials:
Tubular gauze or knitted cotton 1¼" (3 cm) wide, 4¾" (12 cm) long. Fleece wool, knitted cotton, knitting wool or bits of fur, thin insulated wire 16" (40 cm) long.

Instructions:
Make the head and body from the tubular bandage. Sew on knitting wool for hair, or stick and sew on a fur wig or dark unspun sheep's wool.

As with the seven dwarfs wind the centre of a piece of wire in a loop round the neck. Bend the ends over at the doll's hands and twist the wire back in a spiral to the shoulders. Bend it downwards from the shoulders along the side of the body to the hips and sew the wire firmly on to the body. Make the legs in the same way as the arms, bending the ends over at the toes and twisting the wire back in a spiral to the top of the legs. Sew the ends of the wire

carefully into the lower part of the body, ensuring that no pointed ends are sticking out anywhere (Fig. 82).

Make a body out of wool, laying it round and in among the wire. Sew a piece of knitted cotton round it. Make sure that the ends of the wire are well tucked into the wool. Wrap fleece wool round the arms and legs. Wind thread round the wool to secure, and secure at shoulders and hips (Fig. 83).

Once you have shaped the doll to your liking pull the sewn suit over it all (Fig. 84) and fasten at the neck. Bend the feet forward and sew across the bend.

I should like to suggest that as many children live in a time of surplus and in overstocked playrooms, in order to give the doll's house its proper value as a plaything, it can be put away during the summer and brought out again during the winter months. The novelty can be enhanced by adding a new piece of furniture or a new inmate each Christmas.

19. The hobby-horse

Ride a cock horse to Banbury Cross
To see a fine lady upon a white horse.
With rings on her fingers, and bells on her toes
She shall have music wherever she goes.

One of the oldest toys, the hobby-horse can still be found in the playroom. Though the car has almost completely replaced the horse, still the old rhymes and songs of the rider survive. One sight of a horse and rider can awaken the fascination which throughout the generations has gripped both young and old. So even today little children will go trotting on their hobby-horses — and the power of their imagination turns the stick with the horse's head into a swift and powerful steed (and makes the child and horse one).

When making the hobby horse we must remember that the more finished and perfect it is, the less is left to the child's imagination. So the simpler we leave it, the better.

Materials:
A pole 3 ft (1m) long, ¾" (20mm) diameter, or a shortened broom-stick. Wool for stuffing (or old knitting or material, cut up), a thick sock, 2 yards (2 m) of braid or coloured tape about ¾" (2 cm) wide, several little bells, bits of felt or leather for ears and eyes, bits of fur or thick knitting wool for the mane.

Instructions:
Stuff the foot of the sock tight with wool right up to the heel. Insert the stick to the bottom of the heel. Pack the leg of the sock tight with wool round the stick. Tie the neck of the sock tightly round the pole and hammer a small nail through the heel of the

sock into the pole so that the head will not swivel round (Fig. 86). To get the right shape for the horse's head bend the sock in at the heel and sew along the throat to hold the shape. Shape the nose and mouth by tying with a tight thread (Fig. 88). Secure the 'mane' by sewing along the edge of the piece of fur or if the mane is made of knitting wool, make bundles of loops by winding the wool several times round your hand. Sew the bundles tight on to the centre-line of the head and neck. Cut the loops and the mane will fall neatly to each side (Fig 87). Fix the eyes, ears and harness as in Fig. 89. A felt or cloth collar covers the place where the neck is tied on and makes a nice finishing touch.

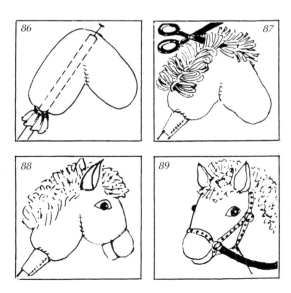

20. Mending dolls

When dolls have been played with and cuddled a lot they begin to look rather dilapidated. Children mind this less than adults who often quietly get hold of the doll to give it a facelift. In the foreword I wrote that it is better not to make the dolls in the children's presence, and the same applies of course to mending.

With my own children I was in the habit of making the dolls disappear two days before Christmas (the children were too taken up with other exciting things) and then the dolls suddenly reappeared by magic on Christmas Eve, all spruced up and with fresh clothes.

I washed the doll, undid the seams and stuffed in more wool. If legs and arms had become loose I sewed them on again.

It was more difficult to renew the faces. If it is at all possible darn the face with thin wool or thread and touch up the eyes and mouth, otherwise take a piece of knitted cotton the size of the face, press it tightly over the old face and secure it with pins before sewing it on with fine stitches (Figs. 90 and 91). Make new eye sockets and make a new neck.

Give the doll new hair, taking care to make the doll as nearly the same as before. With my daughter's favourite doll from her third to her thirteenth year I had to carry out this 'plastic surgery' several times, but despite these 'operations' the doll remained much loved all those years.

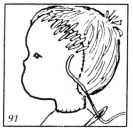